Sacrifice

Sacrifice

poems

Cecilia Woloch

TEBOT BACH

HUNTINGTON BEACH • CALIFORNIA

Acknowledgements

Some of these poems have appeared in the following publications: *The Antioch Review; Zyzzyva; Poetry/LA; ONTHEBUS; Interim; The Wildwood Journal; Sheilanagig; Sculpture Gardens Review; Catholic Girls; Breaking Up Is Hard To Do; Grand Passion: The Poets of Los Angeles and Beyond.*

The author is indebted to the members of Holly Prado's Tuesday morning writing workshop for their support and encouragement, and to her teachers: Holly Prado, Jack Grapes, and JoAnn Bealmear.

FIRST AND SECOND PRINTING CAHUENGA PRESS

ISBN 9781893670198
Library of Congress Control Number: 2005928006

Front cover monoprint "One X One" by Jonde Northcutt
Typesetting by: Greg Boyd
              Melanie Matheson

THIRD PRINTING 2005

A Tebot Bach book

Tebot Bach, Welsh for *little teapot*, is A Nonprofit Public Benefit Corporation which sponsors workshops, forums, lectures, and publications. Tebot Bach books are distributed by Small Press Distribution, Armadillo, Ingram, and Bernhard De Boer.

www.tebotbach.org

For my mother and father

Contents

III.

Teaching the Children's Children to Fly

sac′ ri fice: (Fr. *sacer* sacred + *ficare* to make)
an act of offering something precious to deity

I.

FLIGHT

My mother's dreams were dreams of her children being carried away by a storm. Six of us — where is the seventh? — tied by our waists with a rope to her waist; a daisy-chain of bodies too light to land, we unfurled in the wind. She said it was always spaghetti that kept her awake. She said Italian food spelled nightmares and my father used to work those tepid hours until dawn. How was I blessed to never know my mother was so afraid?

Until one morning I crept out and saw them sitting on the front steps of the house, the light still gray above their heads. My mother in her flowered summer duster and my father in his uniform, dark blue. She must have called him home from work. He must have come — leaving the noise of the runway, the silver monsters we all loved, the DC9's, the cargo planes, the tools so certain in his hands — just to hold her while she cried. To whisper here like this: *Shhh, the kids are all in bed. They'll be all right.*

All but one, who was standing there watching through the screen door, terrified, loved. Knowing that anything could happen, suddenly; knowing the clock on the stove was turned to a time I couldn't tell. Dream time. Their coffee cups. And the way she fit like a blossom into the blossom of his arms. And how I felt the nightmare wind already coming up and couldn't warn them, and how weightless I've become.

The Shock of Creation

A PHOTOGRAPH OF MY FATHER, CIRCA 1949

Behind him, the window is open.
Shadows cross in the grass beneath
the chair he is tipping back.
One is my father's —
the man in the photograph leaning
away from the too-bright sun.
He is dressed in white,
his legs stretched out, his feet
in their heavy black shoes propped up.
But why is he smiling?
This is the prison farm, he is young,
they have sent him to work,
and so recklessly handsome I can't help
loving him, already,
before I am born.
And who is he smiling toward
in the distance, whose shadow
slants into the frame, crossing his?

My father's dark hair is combed to one side;
his hands are folded in his lap.
He could sit like this for the next forty years
but he won't.
The man in the picture is going to stand up
and learn to type
and read hundreds of books
and make airplanes fly
and marry a woman he sees on the South Side of Pittsburgh
and offers a ride in his car.

She will bear him five daughters and two sons.
One of those children will stare at this photograph for years
without ever knowing
what place it is
or the name of that other man
holding the camera —

a prison doctor who'd saved her father
after he broke from the quarry gang, ran
past guards jeering *Russkie, Commie,* buckshot
like hot sleet tearing his skin
and the warden who hissed,
Go ahead, bastard, die —
until he went as far
as the bright edge of it,
then heard the doctor's voice whispering over him,
Don't go, don't leave us yet.

And she'll want to lure him back, herself —
the man in this photograph,
sharp-featured, young,
who is not her father, yet, who has been
resurrected, already, once
and brought by the doctor whose name will be lost
under his wing to the prison farm.
She will want to beg him
never to die, to stay
in that chair tipped above the crossed shadows,
just leaning back with the window behind him,
staring out restlessly at the world.
But I can't stop him —
this is America, prison or not,
and he wants me to live.

TANGIBLE SWEETNESS

Oh God, she's beautiful.

It's New Year's Eve, the dress is pink, she's twenty-one years old. She hasn't seen me yet; she may not even know I'll come. A sour daughter, sickly, difficult, begging her to save the dress and here I am, gone past it. Already older than she was the night she wore it; and right there in her body, crying with her on the steps. What's terrible is I know why she's crying and I can't explain it either.

On the periphery, my father smokes a cigarette. Laughs. Worries.

Through space and time we touch in this thin moment, make a pact: to break jaggedly in three, to live by chance.

There's even music and it's music I will love. An orchestra in black and white, a dance that haunts my body.

Mother, for the pink dress, for each thing that never was. Father, a toast. Gather that woman in your arms, begin my life. It's 1956. This is a waltz.

CONCEPTION

> *. . . love is a drowning in flood water*
> (anon., Irish, 9th Century)

First, we were triplets —
my mother and father and I
They were born starving
I was born thin
We all smelled of prison and cabbage and cigarette smoke
We began to divide in our dreams

I was the lizard who broke from their skin
I was the crack in the egg of their sleep
I was the dark head that nested between them
the daughter with strong teeth who bit through the cord

Who does she look like,
how can she breathe with such tiny arms?

When I started to bleed on my own
I slipped out of the bed —
years ago, years ago, years ago
many thousands of deaths before now

But always, that black moment just before love
when my hair fills with shadow
my hands move through some old, known water again
And what I reach for is too deep to touch —

it's that first drowning
that last splash of light

the silver web torn from my eyes
those lost bodies
my twins

SACRIFICE

My father gives up the red Ram Dodge
for a dark-haired woman, age nineteen.
My mother gives up her job at the A&P.
Streetcars pass, children are born.
My mother is telling me not to cry,
my father weeps.
I marry, become unemployed.
My car gets old.
My husband's smooth fingers slip out of my hand.
My brother arrives in a Thunderbird
with a blonde and a son.
No one has cash.
My sister gives birth
and my sister gives birth
and my sister gives birth.
We are little, we write our names
on each other's backs in soap
in the steamy bath, then wipe them away.
We are grown and we give up our rosaries.
My father steadies his hand,
the letter arrives.
My mother spills mysteries into the telephone,
her kitchen is ceaselessly green.
We love ourselves, we all sink back
in the deep red seats.

EASTER, TRYING MY WINGS

We were strange children who wanted
to fly instead of lie down.
Easter, our buckles shined,
we turned our tilted eyes from the camera.
My dress was blue, I buried tulips
next to the house, where the ground was warm.
Jesus on chocolate crosses, Jesus
there in the palm fronds, the smell
of eggs and bread and cigarette smoke in the kitchen.
This most Sunday Sunday of all.
My brothers, in new clothes, swung
from the young trees, rolled down the yard.
My small sisters danced and danced for the camera.
I am the one in the corner, everywhere, slowly
folding, unfolding her arms.

CABBAGE

My mother's hands are quick.
She stuffs the cabbage leaves with meat and rice,
rolls them into fists.
The pressure cooker screams, its jet of white steam
wets the kitchen.
Work to eat.
My father bowing hungrily,
my brothers growing into men,
My sisters making dainty piles of soggy leaves,
like skin.
At every meal, we eat our mother's hands.
At every meal we thank the gods of cabbage
who are green.

THE PICK

I watched him swinging the pick in the sun,
breaking the concrete steps into chunks of rock,
and the rocks into dust,
and the dust into earth again.
I must have sat for a very long time on the split rail fence,
just watching him.
My father's body glistened with sweat,
his arms flew like dark wings over his head.
He was turning the backyard into terraces,
breaking the hill into two flat plains.
I took for granted the power of him,
though it frightened me, too.
I watched as he swung the pick into the air
and brought it down hard
and changed the shape of the world,
and changed the shape of the world again.

BURNING THE DOLL

I am the girl who burned her doll,
who gave her father the doll to burn —
the bride doll I had been given
at six, as a Christmas gift,
by the same great uncle who once introduced me
at my blind second cousin's wedding
to a man who winced, *A future Miss
America, I'm sure* — while I stood there, sweating
in a prickly flowered dress,
ugly, wanting to cry.

I loved the uncle but I wanted that doll to burn
because I loved my father best
and the doll was a lie.
I hated her white gown stitched with pearls,
her blinking, mocking blue glass eyes
that closed and opened, opened and closed
when I stood her up,
when I laid her down.
Her stiff, hinged body was not like mine,
which was wild and brown,
and there was no groom —

stupid doll,
who smiled and smiled,
even when I flung her to the ground,
even when I struck her, naked, against
the pink walls of my room.
I was not sorry, then,
I would never be sorry —

not even when I was a bride, myself,
and swung down the aisle on my father's arm
toward a marriage that wouldn't last
in a heavy dress that was cut to fit,
a satin dress I didn't want,
but that my mother insisted upon —
Who gives this woman? — wondering, *Who takes
the witchy child?*

And that day, my father was cleaning the basement;
he'd built a fire in the black can
in the back of our backyard,
and I was seven, I wanted to help,
so I offered him the doll.
I remember he looked at me, once, hard,
asked, *Are you sure?*
I nodded my head.

Father, this was our deepest confession of love.
I didn't watch the plastic body melt
to soft flesh in the flames —
I watched you move from the house to the fire.
I would have given you anything.

LUCK

My father could make money multiply in his pockets, that's what we thought. When he napped on the couch, change fell into the cracks — quarters, nickels and dimes — and we dug for it. (We have always been miners for coal, like our grandfathers were, never miners for gold.) And when, in the morning, he slept in their bed after working all night, our mother — getting us off to school, needing money for somebody's lunch — would reach for his pants, crumpled, limp on the floor. And without opening his eyes he would grab her wrist, stop her hand in mid-air. *Caught again,* she would laugh; but she knew he would have enough, and would give it to her.

Our father, provider, the source. The one who could fix anything that broke: our shoes, our bicycles, even our hearts. A mechanic, he knew all the secrets of how things worked; brought home his paycheck in the empty metal lunchbox every week, keeping just twenty dollars for himself. But by Christmas, those twenties were hundreds, and he'd peel them off, give me strict instructions: *Your mother needs boots,* he would say, *a new coat. Buy her anything she wants.*

This was just some of the luck he had, this boy raised in company shacks, sent to school in shirts his mother stitched together from New Deal flour sacks. To hold onto a penny, a nickel, a dime, until it was more than he'd ever had. More than he'd ever dreamed possible. And the rest was us: seven children whose heads he rubbed, whose bare feet he warmed with his hands. *I'm lucky,* he'd say, *I have seven good kids.* Though I am perhaps the most fortunate. The fortunate daughter whose wild hair he brushed and wove into braids but did not try to tame. I remember I'd stand with my palms upturned and watch the coins raining into them. *Is that enough?* he would ask. And it was. It was almost more than I could ever bear away.

THE SHOCK OF CREATION

Everywhere I float in my mother's eyes —
watery, dark, she remembers
I was tiny and calm, I was *perfect*, she says,
my new teeth and the shock of creation.

She is holding her chin in the palm of her hand
and I have turned to her
at the dining room table, at last
we believe one another.

And no one says *tenderly* or *redeeming* or
Father forgive us.
Blurring, we know who we are,
how I've grown nervous and strong
and why she did not rush to save me.

THE SUMMER OF 1969

Mary and I grew up fast
to get where the boys were.
I was twelve, she was sixteen, all summer
we shoplifted eyeshadow, costume jewelry, expensive
bikini underpants — treasure we hid in the green attic bedroom
that slanted our house like a ship.
We leaned from those high windows, solemnly
smoking our cigarettes into the dark.
Gypsies, our mother called us, letting us go
with the keys to the Ford.
I was Mary's Little Sister wherever we went,
instead of my name. The one who followed,
rode shotgun beside her, watching my face in the side-view mirror.
That was the year I started to feel my sharp tongue in my mouth
and my skin had healed.
Mary was blonde, with a waist like a funnel, thighs
spilling out of her cut-off jeans

and nothing could stop us —
not Daddy's strap, not fear, not
Saint Margaret Mary's, which we had forgotten.
I learned to inhale in the shadows behind
Neville Island Roller Rink; stars squeezed out of factory lights.
Boys I didn't know, didn't like,
kissed me in alleys, in strange back seats.
I was twelve, I remember the smells of leather and teeth,
the sense of doom.

By the next summer, Mary was pregnant.
They sent me away to an aunt in Virginia

but it was too late, already, by then;
my childhood was over,
my hair was wild and damp,
the boys in their haunted convertibles beckoned
again and again from the night.

AUNT STEFFIE'S LAUGH

Aunt Steffie when she died passed on
her witch's laugh to me

> *crack of branches*
> *scratch of owls*
> *the moon's sharp feet*

I was a girl of hard thirteen the year
she taught us *deuces wild*
my sister, seventeen, alarmed with child

We played for pennies I remember
how the stacks of copper spilled
across the clean, white tablecloth, the shuffled
whispering of cards

We took refuge in our skinny step-aunt's
narrow red brick house, along
the wrong side of the tracks
between the alleys blue with dusk

> *sanctum*
> *sanctum*
> *from our father's rage*
> *the neighbor's curtained talk*

Aunt Steffie, who protected us
with danger all that fall
— her voice like crackling cellophane —
flicked Pall Mall cigarettes

laughed so hard the night outside
stood at the windows peering in

    rough branch
    soft owl
    October's broken moon

And a baby boy was born
and I grew less afraid of trees
and when Aunt Steffie died she passed
that bracken caw to me

I hear it like the girl inside me sleeping
shook awake

    laughter ringing out
    small fortunes swept up in our arms

THE ALCHEMIST

At thirteen, I was an alchemist:
I knew how the shape of a boy leaning over me
could be changed to the shape of a god.
If I closed my eyes, there became a hand
at the small of my back,
a hand at the wing of my shoulder,
a mouth in the air I could taste with my mouth.

My mother was just coming through the door;
it was afternoon.
The light through the curtains had turned the room gold.

SYNAPSE. FIRE.

I think of those mining towns. Sixty years after the fact, I drive through the hills of Pennsylvania upwards of eighty miles an hour and I think of how they lived. I think of those shacks that my grandmother swept and of my uncle, the darkest one. Though he's been dead for ten years now I think of the boy he must have been. Willy Sapp, who would go to France in the war, change his name to Charles Reynard. But before all of that. Before the nightclubs and white tuxedos and all the booze and platinum blondes. Before the broken-down Italian shoes and the death in a poverty ward. I think of the little boy in a shack his mother hated, a match in his hand. It begins like that. The story I tell myself as the smoky blue hills roll past. *Fast,* I tell him, *fast. Before it's too late, before you're caught, before you're all run out of Russellton.* I think of him turning to watch. His dark face shining in the blaze.

LIGHT & ACHING

(for my grandmother)

Mary, was it sleeping pills
or hanging or the knife?
How strange to see you smiling back at me:
as if you looked into a mirror and then laid
the mirror down —
my face, the frame of false red hair,
the same desire.
Was the light on in the kitchen when you died?
I try to conjure up Detroit in '49.
I dream the great-granddaughter Jenny, as you wished.
Mary, we are wax in one another,
growing warm.
These candles burn tonight,
my hand moves in and out of shade.
Love fiercely, you say;
stand back from the door.

HISTORY

(for Suzy)

To be kept alive by as human a thing as desire. The smell of fresh candles and soap on my hands. People I love are getting old and no one can die for them, no one can help.

I send my prayers out over the lawn chairs, empty of bodies, tonight, in the yard; the moon hanging low. My sister asleep in a motel room by the ocean. Who wonders about our tilted eyes and the mysteries of our father. Why our uncle changed his name, whose name that was *(black sheep, sweet fox)*. And who murdered our father's mother or did she finally murder herself? The sleeping pills, the guns, the bath tub gin, the Tarot cards. Her handsome sons locked up in prisons. And who our father's father was. And why our mother's mother died so young with jaundiced eyes. The gangster Christmases, the neighbor in her black slip at the door, who tried to bet her shoes, her husband's shoes. Which we have all been guilty of. Our grandfather the white tree giving up his mandolin. These secrets rising to the surface to be known and known again.

Getting to the heart of things, where my hand is most afraid. Slicing melon or opening letters; drawing the smoke of the incense in clockwise circles in front of my belly. We come from a long line of fortune tellers, of dreamers of cigarettes, of blue-eyed outlaws and women and men who danced on the slow, dark porch of a big white house that was never asleep. Who rock the bed with impossible love and make their children frightened and sick as we listen between them to the walls. Old and unbroken as they are, still flaunting their scars in the lopsided rooms where all war comes down to this meager breakfast: our history.

Where I fall in the family tree and hang, as a girl, upside down in the branches. All night with my arms in their sockets, dreaming the long Carpathian dreams. My grandmother singing and working the cards. My grandmother yellow with grief. My sister whose fingers turn white from the solemn guitar. That slow, that deep. Gypsies, and makers of doorways.

There is nothing to keep us from throwing ourselves on the mercy of death but desire.

II.

A FEW NOTES
ON ATTRACTION

After all, it must be this. Someone brushes up against you in the dark
and there it is: that tingle of surrender, recognition. How you know
that, this time, when he backs you up into the hedges on the far side
of the door, not to say *I think I love you*, yet. Barely to breathe. To quote
a suicidal poet's villanelle. Or when to put your small face in his jacket's
white lapels and hear a voice you hardly know is your voice telling him
I do. It must be this: that we have always loved the smell of our own
hands on someone's skin; and the first thing in the morning, in the
parking lot of dreams, or in the back seat of his brother's Ford, already
half-asleep, fallen to the body of the words. A parachute, a name. Or
why we choose to dance so late with someone else's love. To feel that
common pulling down. To know that there are many, many gods. And
some of them are whistling to us now, and some are singing. Across a
room becoming dangerous with everything we want.

The White Dress

CUPID'S HUNTING FIELDS

Taste this, he said
and I thought I saw his dark eyes move
through the blindfold.
The field was impossibly gold;
I didn't know my face from the other faces,
my dress from the sky's great dress.

Taste it, he said
and it wasn't my voice that answered,
that said *yes* to him;
but my mouth came open, as if in prayer
and the liquid did not pour into me,
my body poured into the field.

IT'S YOUR WIFE

in her bra and her slip and oh, god
you go to her —
the woman who stands in the mirror,
this fresh-limbed girl
of your very bright morning;
she is half-dressed,
you'll be late for the
ceremony, it's Sunday
and this is your wife.

The guests at the wedding look longingly at her,
the two of you dancing.

Her skirt is the future your future
turns back on:
flaring and simple and pretty and safe
in a way that you never dreamed, smoking and smiling
this hour in magic light;

the geese and ducks bleating,
the old faces haloed,
the holy men calm and all confidence — *this
is the way life is done:*

on your knees
in a suit
at a picnic bench,
everything swirling and amber and finally

cool — this is the apple
your heart sucks to, aching
for something hard and sweet
with a word in it, this
is your wife.

PERSEPHONE, WEDDING NIGHT, LANTERN & SEEDS

Take his dumb fingers,
his swollen palm,
the curve of flesh you've bruised and kissed
and pressed against your mouth.
Now, calmly, in your blue throat,
count the steps
and lead him under.

No tiny birds on wedding cakes have ever flown so deeply.

Through the veil, your scattered breath —
the sparkle of it, heavenly and damp.
Across the white dress, as you lift it
in the tepid wind, dark feathers,
loosely blessed.

Now touch the walls and lick the sweating glass.
Now tell him everything your mother said:

> How it would come to this,
> in rooms you only tested with your sleep;
> how each bright nightmare of your wedding would slip
> down your arms and drown; how
> in this fevered coming-after you would hear
> familiar laughter, taste the wild sting
> of the bitter seed he offers,
> salt and blood.

Now breathe more secretly,
step down.
Spread the shadow of your gown across
the blade of his hot wrist.

Lean forward. Kiss him desperately.

WATCHING HIM SLEEP

Look at him. Look at him sleeping there, like a boy. He's probably dreaming of his dogs, not dreaming of me. Look at the cleft in his chin where the skull came together; I'll put my tongue in that crevice and wake him. No. Watch him stir, watch him breathe. He's hunting for doves, I think; he's trying to murder them quickly. Look how he slings one heavy arm across the dark in search of me. Mother, he isn't gentle. But can you picture his delicate ear, the pale half-moon of his eyelid? Can you see me beside him, awake, burning my eye with his shape until morning?

Mother, I'm saving him up. I'm making a song of his bones to remember.

VOODOO

I hear him downstairs, in the kitchen,
washing dishes.
One pearly strand of blood and mucous trickles
down my thigh.
There goes your son, I think, to him.
There goes your daughter.

I hide the monthly swelling underneath the shapeless sweater
of a dead uncle I loved,
try to camouflage my breasts and hips and thighs.
It doesn't matter, I am visible to him.
I am a mountain in his sleep,
a cat, a monster curled against him,
the one who paints the treeless street
with moonlight, shadow, wind.

How do I tell him, secretly, what he can't know?

He draws my ragged hair, in stiff curls, through his hands.
I break the wishbone of his white arms every night.
And then I eat his heart,
I eat his heart.

RUIN

the kiss falling backwards into the trees
leaning away from the lighted windows

the kiss of the glassy moon in the house
of the translucent plums as they ripen

flesh so thin, it cries in our teeth

how beauty diminishes beauty
kissing whomever we think we might love
and are losing already

oh balance with me on the stairs
who could never hold me
saying, *I have you*

now, in such reckless adoration
and all the sad drapery of our arms

the kiss leaning skyward into the trees

the lit plums like delicate moons
as they fall from our mouths

SPRING,

and no promise of peace. Shallow, human laughter; skin, greedy for light. The glimmering city, the minty trees, the earth giving way underneath us. A helpless season. Dove over dark grass, the watery gray of the air. Now, in our bodies, the fish-like children ache to be seen. Our mouths are translucent. We leap from the red winter, slowly, more cautious; the wind stirs our innocent feet. And though we cannot be new again, we must be new. So that suddenly I meet you, unfold your dark face in my two burning hands. Amazed, in this glory of weather between us, how upright you slant, in such heat. Yellow love that I've poisoned. Poisonous mystery that I eat. Small, blue flame that feeds me. Hercules. Spring.

THE OPEN DOOR BACK
INTO THE WORLD

Oh sweet verandah
this time he's given me up for good
the honeymoon door in and out of the bedroom
the last swung darkness

eternally smoking a cigarette
with his eyes closed

This time he's given me up for good
and my twelve rotting roses
the cold, small foot in his white heat of dreams

and painted the windows
and swept up the ashes

This time the cake flying over his shoulder
and the car keys and half of his life
which was never expected

the air like a dress he could lift with his hands

And under the balcony
where he strikes a match

the thrown cat, the bride in the bathroom

oh glass, oh glass, oh glass
he has given me up

VOW

I do, I did, I loved you and the snapping back and even then, it's true.
The day I cried out for my rings, laughing and thin, and you were not
beside me, anywhere, but still the stiff belief, the satin dress. Because
you guessed I guessed your future, ripe with children, distant, calm,
when all along you loved the gypsy, didn't you? She called the storm
up, right on time, and all the colors you'll remember years from now.
The sudden green that hit the sky, the gorgeous thunder. Our families
silent in the pews and I was saying, yes, I do and yes, I wouldn't and
I did and who you saw and heard and straddled you, that night, that
drunken bride — she gives you back your hand, your ring, your heart.

GODS OF THE SWEET
BURNING CEDAR

We who believed in the untender faith
that comes at the edge of a room
that had seemed to be empty, and entered it.
We who made love on the roof in the sun
in the middle of summer, mid-day
under a sky full of airplanes and telephone lines,
each body a mouth and naked except for our hands.
We who passed one another in shadow,
whose shadows spread under the cracks of doors;
the smoke from my cigarette in your eyes,
your smoke in my hair.
We who cooked three eggs on Sundays
and read the black news in our two wooden chairs.
We who shattered the silences
with wine glasses, telephones, ashtrays,
our faces gleaming like Jack 'o Lanterns
in one another's dreams.
We of the signs on the freeways not pointing home,
your angels unknown to me,
my angels unholy and strange to you.
We who betrayed the dim saints of our mothers and fathers,
who lost all religion
in one hundred nights, more or less, of our lives.
My fingers are bitter and small.
The candles you gave me, the final green,
burn to the last
as I pray, miles away from you now
as I pray to the vast gods of loneliness
as I kneel in my white house and pray.

CONSOLATION

It doesn't count as a swan if the white car flies over a cliff in the dream. The eggs you've eaten in silence don't count as eggs that will wreck your heart. It doesn't count as your hand when the smoke from a cigarette curls through the fingers. Your mother's lamb has its breakfast of song and its dinner of poisonous apple. One howl and you turn into paper. It doesn't count as a trick of god for the thing to fly in if the window was open. It doesn't count as god if the swan is a woman and not on fire.

WHITE GOAT, MY EYE
IN ITS CUP

I miss him in bed

the locking, unlocking of arms and legs
the bodies we dreamed with
his white back, his narrow chest
the nightly forgiveness
for what we had done and not done
the blindness, the absence of longing
the ache toward sleep

I miss his mouth in my hair
and his nervous turning
toward me
his turning away
the dark pulling down
of the childish gods
(more boy and girl there
than woman and man)

that room, the whole universe
tipping and flat
the poisonous street light
that poured in
that always poured in

his skin smelled of smoke
my breath stank of wine

we had given up everything, then
but this death grip we held
to each other
as if it were life
as if it were life itself
slowly slipping

the truth with its big teeth
stared in the windows
I hid my face in his neck
we whispered: *I love you*
                    I love you

as if the ceremony of locking, unlocking
could keep out what stood at the door

> the dangerous morning
> the penitent kisses
> the bowing in water
> the drifting apart

EL COMPADRE

Why do we keep coming back to this restaurant?
This is the same red, dimly-lit room
where we sat at a table, years ago
the first time you said that you wanted to leave me.
We shared a booth but our hands didn't touch.
You told me you wanted out of the movies, I saw
you looking off into your life
and you didn't look happy.
We planned our wedding here, years after that,
and we've kept coming back to plan our divorce.
We're not getting anywhere, it seems.
The same horrible doll-faced man is still selling flowers
from table to table, still haunting you.
I still ask for drags of your cigarette —
perhaps an excuse to reach for your hand — you say
old habits are hard to break and we order
one more beer to split.
The food is late and we're always
hungrier than we'd thought.

Tonight, the place is swarming with matriarchs.
You count the old women staggering past us,
their grown children leaning on their arms
or walking behind them, in stiff procession.
I watch you give up the dream of our children.
I watch you turn again to the kitchen and reach
for another cigarette —
this is the magical cue, we have always believed,

for our meal to arrive.
And when it comes, I dip my fork
into your *salsa verde*, your *enchilada*, amazed
that food somehow tastes better from your plate.
And this time we mean it, it's over,
though I wish you were sitting closer to me
and the music were not so loud.
Then I could tell you how, maybe, forever
I will always love you again,
some warm summer night down in Mexico, sprawled
on the beach where you're kissing my eyes
and the salt we taste is the salt of each other
and tomorrow and honeymoon.
And here we are, always falling, though the years
and our appetites change, into the same sea,
El Compadre — where the waiters forget
what we came for but know
who we are.

TIN

I snagged against my love and then I married him for the ragged tin
of his arms. For his bulletproof heart. For his shocking hair. Every
night of our marriage we dreamt and woke with the taste of the sea
in our mouths. The sea which is grey in this part of the world, when
it isn't green. A handsome man with a spine I could kiss like I once
kissed the beads of the rosary or the links in a chain link fence.
Because I believed what I read with my lips: that between what we
love, we are loved. And the sparks of silver we see from the corners
of our eyes when there's nobody there are not hallucinations, at all,
but trails of light from one world to the next. That's what I mean when
I say: *I have given him up.* That he got away.

THE BACK ROOM, YAMASHIRO

How handsome we are in this empty room —
you with your cigarettes in the pocket of
your leather jacket again, and I
in the perfume of unfaithfulness that follows me everywhere.
I have loved too many men, therefore I could not
love any of them.
The busboys in short red coats seem sure of this.
The waitresses glide back and forth like swans
in their glowing kimonos.
And only this one table left, near the window, only
this one candle burns.
The bare floor shimmers as if we might dance, still
husband and wife, some long honeymoon —
my black sweater loose, so my breast
slips too easily into your hand.

As if only kissing is where kissing
stops — our bright bodies caught
in the dark glass leaning
toward one another, pure light, startle us;
the Japanese lanterns of losses strung high
in the sky of the city at night.

Oh love, to have come this far and not
disappeared. The restaurant floating on top of the hill,
the whole garden hissing as we
step down.

YOUR BACK

I didn't know how much I'd love how you finally look, turning away. Your narrow back and well-timed shoulders. The word *suicidal* falling from somebody's mouth and the overcoat you bought, that first Christmas, when you met me at the airport in New York. Walking slowly through the holiday crowd toward me. Too slowly, already. Too slowly, then. And I couldn't have even imagined kissing my own hands or how forgiveness moves both ways. I slept against you once and your back was cool: that comforted me. The tiger lilies once a week and the long, deep suppers on Sunday nights. The post-coital stroll. Not knowing the lights in those windows we passed had also been set in motion. That I would somehow love to lose you. That you would turn your back, deliberately, in a wild and aching kindness. Leaving me speechless and numb and brilliant. Leaving the word for your name like salt on my tongue and the ghost of your body as witness. And how I would run.

NEW LOVE

There is the white field of his bed
our two small mouths
the dream of pressure.
You are nowhere in the room this winter
calling no one's name.
And I wouldn't call it love, not yet
this bright thirst for his body where my legs
have come unwed
or how the chemicals of who we are, like poppies
burn the air.

You'd watch me cross into the doorway
cross away.
Forgetting, as you always could forget
that every kiss is magical
that the white dress leaping into flames
was also your white dress.

III.

CAUGHT FIRE

The children smell better to us in the morning. Look how their mothers have combed their hair. The light from the sidewalk shines into their eyes and the light on the tops of their heads is more tender than we've ever been to them. They are coming to school from their dreams and their half-finished breakfasts; they are running to stand in lines while the bells split the air and our voices behind them are waving good-bye. The children's skin smells of bathwater, apples, their mothers' last kisses, mistaken perfumes. By noon, they will smell like animals more easy to recognize. Of salt and asphalt and the answers they have been taught to believe are true. But in the morning, the children carry the sun on their backs. Look how their hair shines with it, and their arms. Look at the way we have all caught fire.

Teaching the Children's Children to Fly

IL PLEUT

Time poured down — like rain, like fruit.
—Sinkichi Takahashi, "Time"

(for Carine)

It rains
and this should have been Paris.
Dawn, like a masochist.
Small boys with breadcrumbs, their dark heads
gathered around our knees.

It rains
and the windows go sour,
the baby thinks, *bird*
and I point to the sky that's torn
where a tree comes over the roof.

It rains
and the men in their overcoats look forlorn,
as we slice yellow fruit,
hold our arms to our sides
with the weight of our hands.

It rains
and you pack up the dresses you saved
for the winter that never comes.
Two women, no longer young,
stand in the door,

feed themselves to the air.

STARS IN THE MOUTH OF THE WOLF

(for Heather Douglas)

Los Angeles. Winter burns into spring.
A blue jay has come to live in the bristling tree
at my kitchen window.

Hundreds of miles up the coast, a woman I love is growing thin.
Transparent. Cancer. And the sky shows through her hands.

We believe we will live forever until
we can't believe it again.

At midnight, I wash my blood-soaked lingerie
in the bathroom sink.
The water turns a muddy brown. The body's rust.

What good is it to pray to the medicine moon for happiness?

I have seen stars in the mouth of the wolf.
I know that hope is as sharp as our teeth.

HITTING IT LUCKY

(the blue heron dream)

A blue heron swoops and hovers. Two old women stand gazing up; their long, white hair loose in the radiant wind. When I taste a strand of that hair, coarse and wild, I know I am one or the other of them. The heron a sign to us that *we'll live;* that I've already lived to be one hundred.

There is everywhere magic we knew to expect. We turn in time to see fish with small silver wings, kite-gods, crossing the sky. The sky which is both air and water now. The woman beside me — my great-aunt or mother, my twin — is also one hundred years old. We stand at this shoreline in thin blue dresses. The sea is warm though a hymn of mountains rises beyond us, covered in snow. Over that border, the breathless casinos of Reno or Vegas.

Hitting it lucky. Suddenly knowing that whatever happens will happen twice. To come to a room where music is practiced with others who love us, a long way from home. We have all just woken, laughing, from dreams and wearing this morning each other's robes. My cousins, my mother's sister's children, and I. My name in the song that's been written for me. *Heron:* a bird that wades and flies, from the root *to creak, to cry, to scream.*

I understand that these words are final. That I have arrived to hear them sung.

THE HAIRCUT

First, I brush the waterfall of black hair down his back.
It lets go its pony smell,
gathers its night between my hands.
I hold the scissors like a prayer and close my eyes:
let us relinquish what we've lost,
my first husband, his first wife —
and then I pull it taut and cut
once straight across, one finger's length,
one of my fingers, which are small
and then I give the lock to him.
That's all? he says,
as if this were too easy and too quick.
So then I trim the fine dark hairs along his neck.
He bows his head.
Click, click, click. The candle burns.
I stand behind him in the kitchen, say,
My grandmother did this.
He's sitting on the high stool like a boy I might have loved.
Was she a witch? he asks
and *Yes,* I say, *of course.*
And then I do not want to put the scissors down
or break this spell.

Later, we embrace beneath the jagged map of stars
on Second Street; the moon is half.
Faint constellations dizzy us.
We hold each other hard and do not fall.
Each kiss is sharp.
I have the scissors in my purse, the night is young,
it smells like grass.

TOM

To have been held around the hips and had it whispered to you, *oh girl.* A man who is less than your lover but more than your friend at four a.m., when you stand on the steps leading up to the bedroom and he stands below. To have revealed ourselves so well in all the talk between cigarettes, in our stocking feet as we turn to go to our separate beds, that we hate to go. Let's call it a night. Let's call it a night among old friends and sleep past noon. Let's call it a night in the house on the hill where Tom lives alone when there's nobody here. Let's call him Tom because I have never called him any other name, in all these years not Tommy or Thomas or Sweetheart or Dear or God Bless You, Goodnight. Because he has called me *girl* and the word is his hand at the small of my back. And his name is his face against my chest, not hard but drawn tight as the skin of a drum. And the rooms in which we won't be able to fall asleep till dawn have such thin walls that we'll hear the racing of each other's hearts and forget we're not young.

WEATHER

There is this thread which is really nothing
but seems to be holding us all together —
let's call it the weather of God:
how, mysteriously, you draw someone you hoped
you had lost back into your life,
or maybe he's asked for you, for unknown
reasons of his own.
Anyway, there you are in your sunglasses, saying
you don't remember, saying
that wasn't you who threw bricks
at his back door, years ago.
It was someone else, and her hands were tied.
Then you turn away and pretend to go,
but the air is suddenly knotted.
You can't move forward,
some death has your heart.

TENDERNESS

All these years these men have woven themselves back and forth like
two threads in my life. One draws the other in, then draws away. I
trace their ghosts on my lips with my tongue, as if I am trying to
decide. Though, of course, I can't have either of them. They are
neither one real enough to love. Not in the sense of flesh and blood
— they are flesh and blood — but as separate men. Which is, after all,
what it is to want: the sharpness of difference to rub up against. And
these two men are twin in my heart. So that even the evenings I wear
the bright dress, drop into the lap of one of them, shifting the weight
of my body to his, the bodies fed and supple with wine, I am aching
for him on the other side. The other one. Someone is always missing
no matter who is making love. This is why I can't be kissed without
kissing back. Because the tenderness is all in the absence, and one man
lifts my wrist to his mouth while the other sighs into my hair.

SLEEP. NOT FALLING. YET.

And then your body as ravine
and I am slipping to the edge of it —
you ask if there are trees, I say
a few.
And moonlight through the alley throws itself onto the bed.
My eyes are closed, my eyes are opened,
it's the same no matter how hard I am trying
not to look;
steep green — *Is there a stream?* you ask.
I say that there must be,
though it seems hidden,
maybe underground or maybe in the sky.
And you tell me you hear voices just before you fall asleep
and I say, *Listen to me, listen,*
please don't worry;
and the darkness shifts around us
and the temple in the mountain cracks its door
and we go in.

MAN

Think of him as metaphor, not man. The kiss not flesh but burned
into translucence. That was not your mouth on his and yet it was. And
something else. The mouth of some mute child, some other hunger.
Otherness. Think of him as what you wrecked yourself against
because the one who loves the wreckage wanted it. Wanted the broken
glass of promises with which to prick herself. Think of him as heat and
breath, as naked angel bending down to hold you to the flame. Think
of him as penance for your sins. Sins of omission, of desire. Kneel
down to the memory of him; repent, give thanks. Think of him as
messenger, not man. In the bible of your hands, the gods of touch, the
blood applauds. Longing is all mystery and faith. Remember that.

AT THE B-1 GALLERY

I am standing in open air on a winter night
with my new ex-husband.
We both wear overcoats, hold bottles of beer,
lean slightly toward one another.
The courtyard hums with the voices of friends —
ridiculous, still, how our lives intersect
in spite of whatever arrangements we make to go on.
A reception tonight for the artist
who first introduced us, when we were all young,
who throws one arm around each of us, winks,
and then disappears in the glittering crowd.
We've come here separately, alone,
but can't help being drawn to the same pool of light.
He tells me his mother is going to die and so
I touch this body she made —
under the coat, a sweatshirt worn thin
and under the sweatshirt, his skin
and under the skin the muscle and bone of a man
I have never been sure how to want;
his heart still strange to me, after seven years.

Then it's just like it always was:
he lights my cigarette, I shift back and forth
from one high-heel to the other.
And everyone sees us kissing goodnight
by the side of my car on a downtown street;
they are smiling their sideways smiles as they pass,
all the shop windows lit up with Christmas again.

But I make a u-turn, circle home
to my own dark apartment, a few miles from his,
where I write these words as if I could scratch
through the surface of love, touch the wound
where he lives.

THE INTEGRITY OF ANGELS

Sometimes you wait for the angels to come and they never arrive. In spite of your candles and bells, your white curtains, the windows left open to sky. The phone rings at midnight; a friend is calling you to say that she cannot cry. And you have no words to break the spell for her, small comfort, little advice. Though you've studied eastern religions and ancient rites for clues to your own strange heart — which is, after all, only muscle and blood. You've called on the spirits of everyone you have ever loved who has ever died. But, in fact, they are simply gone, and will not come back from wherever it is they have disappeared into, and will not speak or touch your arm. Sometimes you want proof that there is more to God than the fairytales; everyone does. You want visitations from that other world to tell you what it's like. If there are apples or hunger there, music and graves and light. If the body misses itself and its complex desires, its fevers, its weight. You want an angel who looks like you looked before you were a child to descend again. To hover between what you are, what you dream, and give you the secret of your life. An answer, a promise, your fate in a shining bowl ripe to be eaten at last. But the angels won't come. They want you to decide.

EL COMPADRE, AGAIN

This has the strength of irony:
you're sitting next to me in our favorite
Mexican restaurant — *El Compadre, The Compatriot,*
my husband, my countryman —
saying, the funny thing is, how their daughter's birth
has brought your brother and his wife together,
finally, after nine years.

Child as savior, I nod my head.
We've lived apart for seven months and tonight
we're supposed to be talking divorce, but I
have been thinking of my own childhood —
mother, father, holy ghost — and you
have been thinking about the civil war again.

Your great-great grandfather, Lee's lieutenant,
saved by the hard tack biscuit he kept
in a pocket over his heart from Yankee bullets.
I suggest you erect an altar to bread, without which
you wouldn't be here.

Your wouldn't be here in this dim room to tell me
about your great-grandfather going mad,
waking up one day after three straight shifts
in the cotton mill, a changed man.
Somber. The family somberness gets into you.

And a grandmother on your father's side,
crazy from sugar or just plain crazy,
who played the piano in her dark rages
for days and days without stopping.

On my side, *displaced persons,* immigrants:
the family secrets are poverty, hunger,
suicide, sleeplessness.

One grandmother made bathtub gin
and married three times; the other booked numbers.
Both of them died before they hit fifty,
before your time, as my father says.

And my father's father, already a ghost
before my father was born.
And my mother's father, the white tree,
just whitened away.

Tonight there is nothing between us:
salt and drink and our naked hands.
If I kissed you, would I catch cold?
If you leaned into me in this red booth
slid your long pianist's fingers, your soldier's palms
under my blouse, up my brown gypsy back,
my breath warm with liquor and luck, would the room
fill with children?

Would the waiters stand speechlessly watching,
marvelling, finally, at love's strength and madness,
and then could we reach back and save the others,

gather them up, make a history
that would fit, that would hold all of us?

As I picture this, you are gentle and fierce;
you are holding my wrists, I am teaching
the children's children to fly.

A WOMAN GROWN
BEAUTIFULLY OLD

Some nights in the cave of the tigers,
a woman goes in to be near their sleep.
She doesn't bring jewels,
their teeth are enough.
What she wants is to hear their terrible breathing,
to stand at the mouth of the cave
with the sky on her shoulders,
her face in the heavier darkness.
Her hands drop like stones in a lake to her sides,
her arms are bare.
This is what fearlessness is, and hope:
that the tigers are dreaming of her
as she dreams of them,
that her death has no footprints.

SECOND COMMUNION

"...I am not empty/I am open"
— *Tomas Transtrommer, "Vermeer"*

The girl in the field, her mouth full of flowers,
is eating fresh violets, which taste of rain.
She has forgotten where hunger comes from, other than joy.
The delicate petals dissolve on her tongue;
she fills her hands up with purple again.
She can eat and eat and never displace desire,
never stop wanting more of this watery flesh.
Second Communion. This time the god loves her back.

DADDY'S TATTOOS

I touch the tattoo on his arm
— a shrunken heart, a blur of blue-black ink —
and I touch the tattoo on his fist,
the one that says *Ginny* in loving script,
and try to remember who she was:
an old girl-friend, the red-head, I think,
whose picture hung over his bed, years in prison,
so that she is also a part of us, now,
one of our legends, our myths.

And I would kiss his tattoos if I could,
kiss the young sailor who offered his arm to the needle,
his heart to the fiery girl,
kiss the words I can no longer read
tattooed onto his skin, the whole story of him.
I would kiss every mark on my father's body:
the wreath of flowers burned into his wrist,
even the buckshot still dark in his lungs
where it blossomed inside him, no way out —

if the room weren't so bright, if the hospital bed
were not so rigid with sleek metal rails,
and the doctor, half-smiling, were not watching us
as I turn to my father, in tears, and he asks
as if startled, just seeing me here,
Hey, why are your eyes getting red?
— the first clear words he has spoken in hours —
and the bars, the bars come down
as he says, *Oh my baby,* reaches with one hand,
draws my head toward his chest.

UNCLE FRANK

("del Segro" — the end of the song)

Uncle Frank takes off his cap and asks the good lord to help him out.
He is fixing a lawnmower, or a bike, or some old stereo he calls *a
Victrola* and rescued from the trash. He is eighty-one and he's wearing
pants last patched by the hands of his years-dead wife. He lives alone
except for the dog in the yard who sleeps under his bed at night. That
sweet-faced bitch whose scratching he once mistook for another heart
attack. And so we laugh with him — my mother and father and I, and
Uncle Paul. And my sister who sits at our great uncle's feet, which are
long, like his fingers: humble, thick. I think of that girl who hung
herself, so young and pregnant with his child. I think of the beautiful
woman he married who went to fat, who died of rot. I watch Uncle
Frank spit streams of tobacco juice from his mouth into a jug. The
very man who long ago walked so many miles to simply work that he
fainted from hunger near the tracks. And I wonder if any life goes far
enough to ever heal itself. To be fixed in memory, at least. My uncle
Frank who does repairs in the dark garage beneath this room. Who
feeds the dog, gives things away. Looks into my father's dim eyes,
hard, saying, *My hands shake, too, sometimes. If you can make it work,
it's yours.*

And when he can't, when his fingers slip, he offers his bare head up
to god. As if those crucifixes nailed to every wall could answer him.
And the engine chokes itself awake, the motor hums, the needle drops
by some stiff miracle exactly into the middle of the last notes of the
song.

TENDING OUR FATHER

I sit on the hospital bed
watching him sleep in the tipped-back chair;
one brother and one of my sisters, far
on the other side of the room.
Sunday: the t.v.'s numb eye,
the crossword puzzle, the candy we've brought.
We tend him as tenderly as we can,
our father who dreams his life over again,
his mouth trembling around some lost word.
I ask for a blanket and cover him.
When he wakes, we'll help him to lift himself
from the chair onto the bed.
I'll look into his eyes to see where he's gone:
our father who carried us in his arms,
in our little sleep, to the safest place.
He'll wave one empty hand over his head,
feeling for heat, ask,
What prison is this?

THE PATRIARCH

We are trying to get a picture of ourselves, while we still can. But there are so many of us now — the photographer laughs and squeezes us in. Shoulder to shoulder, each body so much like the next and each face the dark mirror again. My mother and father pose at the center; we've brought Daddy out of the house in his sweater to sit like the patriarch. Here on the lawn, surrounded by us. One of the grandchildren starts to cry, then the others begin, one by one; Daddy smiles. He smiles from the eye of the storm with his eyes almost closed and his palms on his thighs. We think he's too far away to see, too lost in his memory to come back. But he understands what's going on: we are trying to capture ourselves, full of loss. We ary trying to hold still long enough for an image to form of the way we add up. Though, of course, we multiply. The grandchildren wail, then set free, they all fly. And we open our arms to ourselves and ourselves and lift the smallest ones into the air. My father stands with his arms at his sides, watching us. Even the grass is still young.

CECILIA WOLOCH

was born in Pittsburgh, Pennsylvania, and grew up there and in Kentucky, where she attended Transylvania University and earned degrees in English and Theatre Arts. A resident of Los Angeles since 1979, Ms. Woloch has been active as a poet-in-the-schools and teacher of creative writing workshops. She has received grants for her work in the community from the California Arts Council and the Los Angeles Cultural Affairs Department, and has been the recipient of poetry prizes from *The Wildwood Journal, Literal Latte,* and the Kentucky Arts Council. She spends part of each year travelling and teaching throughout Europe.

Greatful Acknowlegement to the following patrons who made this collection possible: Lillian Lovelace, John and Billie Maguire, Lori Schoenlaub, Cynthia Sears and Frank Buxton

THE TEBOT BACH MISSION

The mission of Tebot Bach is to strengthen community, to promote literacy, to broaden the audience for poetry by community outreach programs and publishing, and to demonstrate the power of poetry to transform life experiences through readings, workshops, and publications.

THE TEBOT BACH PROGRAMS

1. A poetry reading and writing workshop series for venues which serve marginalized populations such as homeless shelters, battered women's and men's shelters, nursing homes, senior citizen daycare centers, Veterans organizations, hospitals, AIDS hospices, and correctional facilities, and for schools K-College. Participating poets include: John Balaban, M.L. Liebler, Patricia Smith, Dorianne Laux, Laurence Lieberman, Richard Jones, Arthur Sze, and Carol Moldaw.

2. A poetry reading and writing workshop series for the community Southern California at large. The workshops feature local, national, and international teaching poets. Participating poets include: David St. John, Charles Webb, Wanda Coleman, Amy Gerstler, Patricia Smith, Holly Prado, Dorothy Barresi, W.D.Ehrhart, Tom Lux, Rebecca Seiferle, Suzanne Lummis, Michael Datcher, B.H. Fairchild, Cecilia Woloch, Chris Abani, Laurel Ann Bogen, Sam Hamill, and David Lehman.

3. A publishing component in order to give local and national poets a venue for publishing and distribution.

Grateful acknowledgement is given to our supporters who make our programs possible and to Golden West College in Huntington Beach, California

TEBOT BACH • HUNTINGTON BEACH • CALIFORNIA
WWW.TEBOTBACH.ORG